50 Global Grains: Beyond Rice and Pasta Recipes for Home

By: Kelly Johnson

Table of Contents

- Quinoa Salad with Roasted Vegetables (Peru)
- Couscous with Lemon and Herb Chicken (Morocco)
- Millet and Vegetable Stir-Fry (India)
- Buckwheat Pancakes with Blueberry Compote (Russia)
- Farro Risotto with Mushrooms (Italy)
- Sorghum and Black Bean Chili (United States)
- Barley and Lentil Soup (Middle East)
- Amaranth Breakfast Porridge (Africa)
- Freekeh Salad with Pomegranate and Feta (Middle East)
- Teff Injera Bread (Ethiopia)
- Wild Rice Stuffed Acorn Squash (Native American)
- Spelt Pasta with Tomato and Basil (Italy)
- Sesame Ginger Brown Rice Bowl (Asia)
- Bulgur Pilaf with Chickpeas (Middle East)
- Kamut Tabbouleh Salad (Lebanon)
- Soba Noodle Stir-Fry with Tofu (Japan)
- Amaranth and Sweet Potato Patties (Latin America)
- Sorghum Porridge with Berries (Africa)
- Freekeh and Roasted Vegetable Skewers (Middle East)
- Polenta with Roasted Vegetables and Pesto (Italy)
- Barley and Mushroom Risotto (Europe)
- Quinoa-Stuffed Bell Peppers (South America)
- Millet Porridge with Coconut Milk (Asia)
- Buckwheat Galettes with Ham and Cheese (France)
- Sesame Seared Tofu with Brown Rice (Asia)
- Farro and Roasted Beet Salad (Italy)
- Spelt Bread with Avocado and Tomato (Europe)
- Teff Porridge with Berries and Almonds (Ethiopia)
- Amaranth and Spinach Stuffed Mushrooms (Global)
- Wild Rice and Cranberry Pilaf (North America)
- Sorghum and Vegetable Curry (Africa)
- Quinoa and Black Bean Enchiladas (Latin America)
- Millet and Sweet Potato Patties (Global)
- Barley and Roasted Vegetable Pizza (Italy)
- Freekeh and Chickpea Salad (Middle East)

- Buckwheat Soba Noodles with Miso Broth (Japan)
- Spelt and Herb Focaccia Bread (Italy)
- Teff Pancakes with Maple Syrup (Ethiopia)
- Sorghum and Pumpkin Soup (Africa)
- Quinoa and Kale Stuffed Bell Peppers (South America)
- Millet and Black Bean Tacos (Latin America)
- Barley and Lentil Stew (Middle East)
- Amaranth and Vegetable Curry (Global)
- Farro and Tomato Bruschetta (Italy)
- Spelt Pasta with Artichoke and Lemon (Italy)
- Teff Injera Tacos with Lentils (Ethiopia)
- Buckwheat Blinis with Smoked Salmon (Russia)
- Sorghum and Peanut Stir-Fry (Africa)
- Quinoa and Roasted Vegetable Buddha Bowl (Global)
- Millet and Banana Breakfast Bowl (Global)

Quinoa Salad with Roasted Vegetables (Peru)

Ingredients:

- 1 cup quinoa, rinsed and drained
- 2 cups water
- 1 medium-sized sweet potato, peeled and diced
- 1 zucchini, sliced
- 1 red bell pepper, chopped
- 1 yellow bell pepper, chopped
- 1 red onion, thinly sliced
- 2 tablespoons olive oil
- Salt and pepper to taste
- 1 teaspoon cumin
- 1 teaspoon smoked paprika
- 1/2 cup cherry tomatoes, halved
- 1/4 cup fresh cilantro, chopped

For the Dressing:

- 3 tablespoons olive oil
- 2 tablespoons balsamic vinegar
- 1 tablespoon honey
- 1 clove garlic, minced
- Salt and pepper to taste

Instructions:

Preheat the oven to 400°F (200°C).
In a medium-sized saucepan, combine the quinoa and water. Bring to a boil, then reduce heat to low, cover, and simmer for 15-20 minutes or until the quinoa is cooked and water is absorbed. Fluff the quinoa with a fork and set aside.
Place the diced sweet potato, sliced zucchini, chopped red and yellow bell peppers, and thinly sliced red onion on a baking sheet. Drizzle with olive oil, sprinkle with salt, pepper, cumin, and smoked paprika. Toss to coat the vegetables evenly.
Roast the vegetables in the preheated oven for 20-25 minutes or until they are tender and slightly caramelized, stirring halfway through.

While the vegetables are roasting, prepare the dressing by whisking together olive oil, balsamic vinegar, honey, minced garlic, salt, and pepper in a small bowl.

In a large bowl, combine the cooked quinoa, roasted vegetables, cherry tomatoes, and chopped cilantro.

Pour the dressing over the salad and toss gently to combine, ensuring all ingredients are well coated.

Allow the salad to sit for a few minutes to let the flavors meld.

Serve the quinoa salad with roasted vegetables either warm or at room temperature. It can be enjoyed as a side dish or a light, refreshing main course.

This Quinoa Salad with Roasted Vegetables brings together the nutty flavor of quinoa with the sweetness of roasted vegetables, creating a wholesome and flavorful dish inspired by the culinary traditions of Peru.

Couscous with Lemon and Herb Chicken (Morocco)

Ingredients:

For the Lemon and Herb Chicken:

- 4 boneless, skinless chicken breasts
- 2 lemons, juiced and zested
- 3 tablespoons olive oil
- 3 cloves garlic, minced
- 1 teaspoon ground cumin
- 1 teaspoon ground coriander
- 1 teaspoon paprika
- 1 teaspoon dried oregano
- Salt and pepper to taste
- Fresh parsley, chopped (for garnish)

For the Couscous:

- 1 1/2 cups couscous
- 1 3/4 cups chicken broth
- 1 tablespoon olive oil
- 1/2 cup raisins
- 1/4 cup slivered almonds, toasted
- Fresh cilantro, chopped (for garnish)

Instructions:

For the Lemon and Herb Chicken:

In a bowl, combine the lemon juice, lemon zest, olive oil, minced garlic, ground cumin, ground coriander, paprika, dried oregano, salt, and pepper to create the marinade.

Place the chicken breasts in a resealable plastic bag or shallow dish and pour half of the marinade over them. Ensure the chicken is evenly coated. Marinate for at least 30 minutes, or refrigerate for a few hours for enhanced flavor.

Preheat the grill or a grill pan over medium-high heat. Grill the marinated chicken breasts for about 6-8 minutes per side or until fully cooked and has a nice char. Cooking time may vary depending on the thickness of the chicken.
Once cooked, let the chicken rest for a few minutes before slicing it into strips.

For the Couscous:

In a saucepan, bring the chicken broth and olive oil to a boil.
Stir in the couscous, cover the saucepan with a lid, and remove it from heat. Let it sit for 5 minutes to allow the couscous to absorb the liquid.
Fluff the couscous with a fork and stir in the raisins and toasted slivered almonds.

Assembling the Dish:

Place a generous portion of couscous on each plate.
Top the couscous with slices of the grilled lemon and herb chicken.
Garnish the dish with fresh parsley and chopped cilantro.
Serve immediately, and enjoy this delightful Moroccan-inspired couscous with lemon and herb chicken, rich in flavor and texture.

Millet and Vegetable Stir-Fry (India)

Ingredients:

- 1 cup millet, rinsed and drained
- 2 cups water
- 2 tablespoons vegetable oil
- 1 teaspoon mustard seeds
- 1 teaspoon cumin seeds
- 1 onion, thinly sliced
- 2 carrots, julienned
- 1 bell pepper (any color), thinly sliced
- 1 cup broccoli florets
- 1 cup snap peas, trimmed
- 2 cloves garlic, minced
- 1-inch piece of ginger, grated
- 2 tablespoons soy sauce

- 1 tablespoon rice vinegar
- 1 tablespoon sesame oil
- 1 teaspoon chili flakes (adjust to taste)
- Salt and pepper to taste
- Fresh cilantro, chopped (for garnish)

Instructions:

In a medium-sized saucepan, combine the millet and water. Bring to a boil, then reduce the heat to low, cover, and simmer for 15-20 minutes or until the millet is cooked and water is absorbed. Fluff the millet with a fork and set aside.

In a large wok or skillet, heat vegetable oil over medium-high heat. Add mustard seeds and cumin seeds, allowing them to splutter.

Add the thinly sliced onion and sauté until translucent.

Add julienned carrots, bell pepper slices, broccoli florets, and snap peas to the wok. Stir-fry the vegetables for 5-7 minutes or until they are crisp-tender.

Create a well in the center of the vegetables and add minced garlic and grated ginger. Sauté for 1-2 minutes until fragrant.

Incorporate the cooked millet into the vegetable mixture, tossing everything together.

In a small bowl, mix soy sauce, rice vinegar, sesame oil, and chili flakes. Pour the sauce over the stir-fry and toss well to ensure even coating. Season with salt and pepper to taste.

Continue cooking for an additional 2-3 minutes, allowing the flavors to meld.

Garnish the millet and vegetable stir-fry with fresh cilantro.

Serve the stir-fry hot, and enjoy this nutritious and flavorful millet dish inspired by the diverse cuisine of India.

Buckwheat Pancakes with Blueberry Compote (Russia)

For the Buckwheat Pancakes:

Ingredients:

- 1 cup buckwheat flour
- 1/2 cup all-purpose flour
- 2 tablespoons sugar
- 1 teaspoon baking powder
- 1/2 teaspoon baking soda
- 1/4 teaspoon salt
- 1 cup buttermilk
- 1/2 cup milk
- 2 large eggs
- 2 tablespoons unsalted butter, melted
- Cooking oil or butter for greasing the pan

For the Blueberry Compote:

- 1 cup fresh or frozen blueberries
- 2 tablespoons maple syrup
- 1 tablespoon lemon juice
- Zest of 1 lemon

Instructions:

For the Buckwheat Pancakes:

> In a large mixing bowl, whisk together buckwheat flour, all-purpose flour, sugar, baking powder, baking soda, and salt.
> In a separate bowl, whisk together buttermilk, milk, eggs, and melted butter.
> Pour the wet ingredients into the dry ingredients and gently fold until just combined. Be careful not to overmix; a few lumps are okay.
> Let the batter rest for about 10-15 minutes to allow the flours to absorb the liquids.
> Heat a griddle or non-stick skillet over medium heat. Lightly grease with cooking oil or butter.
> Pour 1/4 cup of batter for each pancake onto the hot griddle. Cook until bubbles form on the surface, then flip and cook until the other side is golden brown.

Continue cooking the remaining batter, adjusting heat if necessary.

For the Blueberry Compote:

In a saucepan, combine blueberries, maple syrup, lemon juice, and lemon zest. Cook over medium heat, stirring occasionally, until the blueberries burst and the mixture thickens slightly (about 5-7 minutes).
Remove from heat and let it cool slightly.

Assembling the Dish:

Stack the buckwheat pancakes on a plate.
Pour the warm blueberry compote over the pancakes.
Optionally, garnish with additional fresh blueberries and a drizzle of maple syrup.
Serve immediately and enjoy this delightful Russian-inspired breakfast of buckwheat pancakes with a sweet and tangy blueberry compote.

Farro Risotto with Mushrooms (Italy)

Ingredients:

- 1 cup farro, rinsed
- 4 cups vegetable or chicken broth, kept warm
- 2 tablespoons olive oil
- 1 onion, finely chopped
- 2 cloves garlic, minced
- 8 ounces (about 225g) mushrooms (such as cremini or shiitake), sliced
- 1 cup dry white wine
- 1/2 cup Parmesan cheese, grated
- Salt and black pepper to taste
- Fresh parsley, chopped (for garnish)

Instructions:

In a large skillet or wide saucepan, heat olive oil over medium heat. Add the chopped onion and sauté until translucent.
Add the minced garlic and sliced mushrooms to the skillet. Cook for 5-7 minutes or until the mushrooms are golden brown and have released their moisture.
Stir in the farro, ensuring it's well-coated with the oil and mixed with the mushrooms and onions.

Pour in the dry white wine and cook until most of the liquid has evaporated.
Begin adding the warm broth, one ladleful at a time, to the farro mixture. Allow the liquid to be absorbed before adding the next ladle of broth. Continue this process, stirring frequently, until the farro is tender but still has a slight chewiness. This may take around 25-30 minutes.
Once the farro is cooked, stir in the grated Parmesan cheese, and season with salt and black pepper to taste.
Remove the skillet from heat, cover with a lid, and let it rest for a couple of minutes.
Serve the farro risotto with mushrooms hot, garnished with fresh chopped parsley.
Optionally, you can drizzle a bit of extra virgin olive oi and sprinkle additional Parmesan cheese on top before serving.
Enjoy this Italian-inspired farro risotto as a hearty and flavorful dish, showcasing the wonderful combination of nutty farro and earthy mushrooms.

Sorghum and Black Bean Chili (United States)

Ingredients:

- 1 cup sorghum, rinsed and drained
- 3 cups vegetable broth
- 2 tablespoons olive oil
- 1 large onion, diced
- 3 cloves garlic, minced
- 1 bell pepper (any color), diced
- 1 jalapeño pepper, seeds removed and finely chopped (optional, for heat)
- 1 can (15 oz) black beans, drained and rinsed
- 1 can (14 oz) diced tomatoes, undrained
- 1 cup corn kernels (fresh or frozen)
- 2 teaspoons ground cumin
- 2 teaspoons chili powder
- 1 teaspoon smoked paprika
- 1/2 teaspoon ground coriander
- Salt and black pepper to taste
- Fresh cilantro, chopped (for garnish)
- Avocado slices (for garnish)
- Lime wedges (for serving)

Instructions:

In a medium saucepan, combine sorghum and vegetable broth. Bring to a boil, then reduce heat to low, cover, and simmer for 45-50 minutes or until sorghum is tender. Drain any excess liquid and set aside.

In a large pot or Dutch oven, heat olive oil over medium heat. Add diced onion and cook until softened.

Add minced garlic and diced bell pepper to the pot. Sauté for an additional 2-3 minutes until the vegetables are tender.

Stir in the cooked sorghum, black beans, diced tomatoes, corn, and chopped jalapeño (if using).

Add ground cumin, chili powder, smoked paprika, ground coriander, salt, and black pepper. Mix well to combine.

Pour in additional vegetable broth if a thinner consistency is desired.

Bring the chili to a simmer, then reduce the heat to low, cover, and let it simmer for 20-25 minutes to allow the flavors to meld.

Adjust seasonings according to taste.
Serve the sorghum and black bean chili hot, garnished with chopped fresh cilantro and avocado slices.
Optionally, squeeze lime juice over each serving before enjoying.
This hearty and nutritious chili captures the essence of American comfort food with the unique addition of sorghum, providing a delightful twist on a classic dish.

Barley and Lentil Soup (Middle East)

Ingredients:

- 1 cup pearl barley, rinsed and drained
- 1 cup brown or green lentils, picked over and rinsed
- 2 tablespoons olive oil
- 1 large onion, finely chopped
- 3 carrots, diced
- 3 celery stalks, diced
- 4 cloves garlic, minced
- 1 teaspoon ground cumin
- 1 teaspoon ground coriander
- 1 teaspoon ground turmeric
- 1/2 teaspoon smoked paprika
- 8 cups vegetable or chicken broth
- 1 can (14 oz) diced tomatoes, undrained
- 2 bay leaves
- Salt and black pepper to taste
- Fresh lemon juice (optional, for serving)
- Fresh parsley, chopped (for garnish)

Instructions:

In a large pot, heat olive oil over medium heat. Add chopped onion, carrots, and celery. Sauté until the vegetables are softened, about 5-7 minutes.

Add minced garlic, ground cumin, ground coriander, ground turmeric, and smoked paprika to the pot. Stir well and cook for an additional 2 minutes until the spices are fragrant.

Add pearl barley, lentils, vegetable or chicken broth, diced tomatoes (with their juice), and bay leaves to the pot. Bring the mixture to a boil.

Reduce the heat to low, cover the pot, and let it simmer for about 40-50 minutes or until the barley and lentils are tender.

Season the soup with salt and black pepper to taste. Discard the bay leaves.

If the soup is too thick, you can add more broth or water to reach your desired consistency.

Serve the barley and lentil soup hot, optionally squeezing fresh lemon juice over each serving.

Garnish with chopped fresh parsley for a burst of freshness.
Enjoy this hearty Middle Eastern-inspired soup as a nutritious and comforting dish, rich in fiber and wholesome flavors.

Amaranth Breakfast Porridge (Africa)

Ingredients:

- 1 cup amaranth seeds, rinsed and drained
- 2 1/2 cups milk (dairy or plant-based)
- 1 ripe banana, mashed
- 2 tablespoons honey or maple syrup (adjust to taste)
- 1/2 teaspoon ground cinnamon
- 1/4 teaspoon ground nutmeg
- Pinch of salt
- Fresh fruits (such as sliced bananas, berries, or mango) for topping
- Nuts and seeds (such as chopped almonds or pumpkin seeds) for topping

Instructions:

In a medium-sized saucepan, combine the rinsed amaranth seeds and milk. Bring the mixture to a boil, then reduce the heat to low. Simmer the amaranth, covered, for about 20-25 minutes or until the seeds are tender and the mixture has a porridge-like consistency.

Stir in the mashed banana, honey or maple syrup, ground cinnamon, ground nutmeg, and a pinch of salt. Mix well.

Continue cooking the porridge over low heat for an additional 5-7 minutes, stirring occasionally to prevent sticking.

Adjust sweetness and spice levels according to your preference.

Once the amaranth porridge reaches your desired consistency, remove it from heat.

Serve the porridge warm in bowls.

Top each serving with fresh fruits, such as sliced bananas, berries, or mango.

Sprinkle chopped nuts and seeds, such as almonds or pumpkin seeds, over the top for added texture and nutrition.

Enjoy this nutritious and delicious African-inspired amaranth breakfast porridge to kickstart your day with a burst of flavors and energy.

Freekeh Salad with Pomegranate and Feta (Middle East)

Ingredients:

- 1 cup freekeh, rinsed
- 2 1/2 cups water or vegetable broth
- 1/2 cup pomegranate arils
- 1/2 cup crumbled feta cheese
- 1 cucumber, diced
- 1 cup cherry tomatoes, halved
- 1/4 cup red onion, finely chopped
- 1/4 cup fresh mint leaves, chopped
- 1/4 cup fresh parsley, chopped

For the Dressing:

- 3 tablespoons extra virgin olive oil
- 2 tablespoons pomegranate molasses
- 1 tablespoon red wine vinegar
- Salt and black pepper to taste

Instructions:

In a medium saucepan, combine the rinsed freekeh and water or vegetable broth. Bring to a boil, then reduce the heat to low, cover, and simmer for about 20-25 minutes or until the freekeh is tender and has absorbed the liquid. Fluff with a fork and let it cool.

In a large salad bowl, combine the cooked and cooled freekeh, pomegranate arils, crumbled feta, diced cucumber, cherry tomatoes, chopped red onion, mint leaves, and parsley.

In a small bowl, whisk together the extra virgin olive oil, pomegranate molasses, red wine vinegar, salt, and black pepper to create the dressing.

Pour the dressing over the salad and toss gently to ensure all ingredients are well coated.

Allow the salad to sit for a few minutes to let the flavors meld.

Serve the freekeh salad with pomegranate and feta chilled or at room temperature.

Optionally, garnish with additional fresh mint and parsley before serving.

Enjoy this Middle Eastern-inspired freekeh salad as a refreshing and wholesome dish, featuring a delightful combination of nutty freekeh, juicy pomegranate arils, and creamy feta cheese.

Teff Injera Bread (Ethiopia)

Ingredients:

- 2 cups teff flour (preferably a mixture of white and brown teff)
- 1 cup all-purpose flour
- 3 cups water
- 1/2 teaspoon baking soda
- 1/2 teaspoon salt

Instructions:

Mixing the Batter:
- In a large bowl, combine the teff flour, all-purpose flour, and water. Stir well until you achieve a smooth, lump-free batter. The consistency should be similar to pancake batter.
- Cover the bowl with a cloth and let it ferment at room temperature for at least 12 to 24 hours. The longer fermentation imparts a slightly sour taste to the injera.

Preparing the Batter for Cooking:
- After fermentation, the batter will have small bubbles on the surface. Give it a good stir.
- Dissolve the baking soda and salt in a tablespoon of water and add it to the batter. Mix well.

Cooking the Injera:
- Heat a non-stick skillet or an injera pan over medium heat. You won't need oil, as the batter has a naturally non-stick quality.
- Pour a ladleful of batter onto the hot pan, swirling it around to spread it evenly. The injera should be thin, with a diameter of about 8-10 inches.
- Cover the pan and cook for 1-2 minutes until the edges start lifting and small holes form on the surface.

Serving and Stacking:
- Injera is traditionally served with various stews and dishes. Once cooked, remove it from the pan and let it cool.
- Repeat the process until all the batter is used, stacking the injera on a plate as you go.

Enjoying the Teff Injera:

- Serve the teff injera with your favorite Ethiopian stews, such as Doro Wat (chicken stew) or Misir Wat (red lentil stew).
- Tear off pieces of injera and use them to scoop up the stews, savoring the unique flavor and texture of this Ethiopian staple.

Storage:
- Injera is best enjoyed fresh, but you can store leftovers in an airtight container in the refrigerator for a day or two. Warm them slightly before serving.

Enjoy this traditional Ethiopian teff injera bread as a delightful and versatile accompaniment to a variety of flavorful dishes!

Wild Rice Stuffed Acorn Squash (Native American)

Ingredients:

- 2 acorn squash, halved and seeds removed
- 1 cup wild rice, rinsed
- 2 1/2 cups vegetable broth or water
- 1 tablespoon olive oil
- 1 onion, finely chopped
- 2 celery stalks, diced
- 2 carrots, diced
- 2 cloves garlic, minced
- 1/2 cup dried cranberries
- 1/2 cup pecans or walnuts, chopped
- 1 teaspoon dried thyme
- 1 teaspoon dried sage
- Salt and black pepper to taste
- Fresh parsley, chopped (for garnish)

Instructions:

Prepare the Acorn Squash:
- Preheat the oven to 375°F (190°C).
- Place the halved acorn squash on a baking sheet, cut side up. Drizzle with olive oil and sprinkle with salt and pepper.
- Roast the squash for about 40-45 minutes or until it becomes tender when pierced with a fork.

Cook the Wild Rice:
- In a medium saucepan, combine the wild rice and vegetable broth or water. Bring to a boil, then reduce heat to low, cover, and simmer for 45-50 minutes or until the rice is cooked and the liquid is absorbed.

Prepare the Stuffing:
- In a large skillet, heat olive oil over medium heat. Add chopped onion, celery, and carrots. Sauté until the vegetables are softened, about 5-7 minutes.
- Add minced garlic and cook for an additional 1-2 minutes.

Combine Ingredients:

- In a large mixing bowl, combine the cooked wild rice, sautéed vegetables, dried cranberries, chopped nuts, dried thyme, dried sage, salt, and black pepper. Mix well.

Stuff the Acorn Squash:
- Once the acorn squash halves are tender, carefully fill each half with the wild rice stuffing mixture.

Bake:
- Return the stuffed acorn squash to the oven and bake for an additional 15-20 minutes or until the stuffing is heated through and the flavors meld.

Serve:
- Garnish the wild rice stuffed acorn squash with fresh chopped parsley before serving.

Enjoy:
- Serve the stuffed acorn squash as a delicious and hearty dish, representing the flavors and ingredients found in Native American cuisine. It's a perfect celebration of seasonal and nutritious ingredients.

Spelt Pasta with Tomato and Basil (Italy)

Ingredients:

- 8 oz (about 225g) spelt pasta
- 2 tablespoons olive oil
- 3 cloves garlic, minced
- 1 can (14 oz) diced tomatoes (or use fresh tomatoes, diced)
- 1/2 teaspoon red pepper flakes (adjust to taste)
- Salt and black pepper to taste
- 1/4 cup fresh basil leaves, chopped
- Grated Parmesan cheese for serving (optional)

Instructions:

Cook Spelt Pasta:
- Cook the spelt pasta according to the package instructions in a large pot of salted boiling water until al dente. Drain and set aside.

Prepare the Sauce:
- In a large skillet, heat olive oil over medium heat. Add minced garlic and sauté until fragrant but not browned.

Add Tomatoes:
- Add the diced tomatoes (with their juices) to the skillet. If using fresh tomatoes, you can add a splash of water to create a sauce. Bring the mixture to a simmer.

Season the Sauce:
- Season the tomato sauce with red pepper flakes, salt, and black pepper. Adjust the spice level according to your preference.

Combine Pasta and Sauce:
- Add the cooked spelt pasta to the skillet with the tomato sauce. Toss well to coat the pasta evenly with the sauce.

Finish with Basil:
- Stir in the fresh chopped basil, allowing the flavors to meld for a minute or two.

Serve:
- Divide the spelt pasta with tomato and basil among serving plates.

Optional Toppings:

- Optionally, top each serving with grated Parmesan cheese for an extra layer of flavor.

Enjoy:
- Serve this spelt pasta with tomato and basil immediately, savoring the simple yet delicious combination of flavors inspired by Italian cuisine.

This dish is a celebration of the classic Italian pairing of ripe tomatoes and fragrant basil, combined with the nutty and wholesome taste of spelt pasta. Enjoy the simplicity and freshness of this delightful meal!

Sesame Ginger Brown Rice Bowl (Asia)

Ingredients:

For the Rice Bowl:

- 1 cup brown rice, rinsed
- 2 cups water
- 1 tablespoon sesame oil
- 1 cup broccoli florets
- 1 carrot, julienned
- 1 red bell pepper, thinly sliced
- 1 cup edamame (shelled)
- 1/4 cup green onions, chopped (for garnish)
- Sesame seeds for garnish

For the Sesame Ginger Sauce:

- 3 tablespoons soy sauce
- 1 tablespoon rice vinegar
- 1 tablespoon sesame oil
- 1 tablespoon fresh ginger, grated
- 2 cloves garlic, minced
- 1 tablespoon honey or maple syrup
- 1 teaspoon cornstarch (optional, for thickening)

Instructions:

Cook Brown Rice:
- In a medium saucepan, combine brown rice and water. Bring to a boil, then reduce the heat to low, cover, and simmer for 40-45 minutes or until the rice is tender. Fluff the rice with a fork.

Prepare Vegetables:
- While the rice is cooking, heat 1 tablespoon of sesame oil in a large skillet or wok over medium-high heat.
- Add broccoli, julienned carrot, and sliced red bell pepper. Stir-fry for 5-7 minutes or until the vegetables are crisp-tender.

- Add edamame and continue to stir-fry for an additional 2-3 minutes.

Make Sesame Ginger Sauce:
- In a small bowl, whisk together soy sauce, rice vinegar, sesame oil, grated ginger, minced garlic, and honey (or maple syrup).
- If you prefer a thicker sauce, you can mix in cornstarch. To do this, dissolve the cornstarch in a tablespoon of cold water before adding it to the sauce.

Combine and Toss:
- Pour the sesame ginger sauce over the cooked vegetables in the skillet. Toss everything together until the vegetables are well-coated.

Assemble Rice Bowl:
- Divide the cooked brown rice among serving bowls.
- Top the rice with the sesame ginger stir-fried vegetables.

Garnish:
- Garnish with chopped green onions and sprinkle sesame seeds over the top.

Serve:
- Serve the Sesame Ginger Brown Rice Bowl hot, enjoying the harmonious blend of flavors and textures inspired by Asian culinary influences.

This vibrant and flavorful brown rice bowl is a perfect balance of nutty brown rice, crisp vegetables, and a delectable sesame ginger sauce, creating a wholesome and satisfying Asian-inspired dish.

Bulgur Pilaf with Chickpeas (Middle East)

Ingredients:

- 1 cup coarse bulgur
- 1 ½ cups canned chickpeas, drained and rinsed (or cooked from dried chickpeas)
- 1 large onion, finely chopped
- 2 tablespoons olive oil
- 2 cups vegetable broth or water
- 1 teaspoon ground cumin
- 1 teaspoon ground coriander
- 1 teaspoon paprika
- 1/2 teaspoon cinnamon
- Salt and black pepper to taste
- Chopped fresh parsley for garnish

Instructions:

Sauté the Onions:
- In a large skillet or saucepan, heat olive oil over medium heat. Add the chopped onion and sauté until it becomes translucent.

Add Bulgur and Spices:
- Add the coarse bulgur to the sautéed onions. Stir and cook for 2-3 minutes until the bulgur is lightly toasted.

Spice it Up:
- Incorporate the ground cumin, ground coriander, paprika, and cinnamon to the bulgur mixture. Stir well to coat the bulgur with the spices.

Add Chickpeas:
- Add the drained and rinsed chickpeas to the skillet. Mix them with the bulgur and spices.

Pour in Broth:
- Pour in the vegetable broth or water. Bring the mixture to a boil.

Simmer and Cook:
- Reduce the heat to low, cover the skillet, and et it simmer for about 15-20 minutes or until the bulgur is tender and has absorbed the liquid.

Season and Fluff:
- Season the pilaf with salt and black pepper to taste. Fluff the pilaf with a fork to separate the grains.

Garnish and Serve:
- Transfer the Bulgur Pilaf with Chickpeas to a serving dish. Garnish with chopped fresh parsley.

Optional Additions:
- You can enhance the dish by adding a squeeze of lemon juice or a drizzle of extra virgin olive oil before serving.

Enjoy:
- Serve this flavorful Bulgur Pilaf with Chickpeas as a side dish or a light, satisfying main course. It's a nutritious and delicious representation of Middle Eastern cuisine.

Kamut Tabbouleh Salad (Lebanon)

Ingredients:

- 1 cup kamut wheat, rinsed
- 2 1/2 cups water
- 1 cup finely chopped fresh parsley
- 1/2 cup finely chopped fresh mint leaves
- 1/2 cup cherry tomatoes, diced
- 1/4 cup red onion, finely chopped
- 1/4 cup cucumber, diced
- 1/4 cup extra virgin olive oil
- 1/4 cup fresh lemon juice
- 1 teaspoon ground cumin
- Salt and black pepper to taste

Instructions:

Prepare Kamut:
- In a medium saucepan, combine the rinsed kamut wheat and water. Bring to a boil, then reduce heat to low, cover, and simmer for about 40-45 minutes or until the kamut is tender but still has a chewy texture. Drain any excess water and let it cool.

Chop and Dice:
- Finely chop the fresh parsley and mint leaves. Dice the cherry tomatoes, red onion, and cucumber.

Combine Ingredients:
- In a large bowl, combine the cooked kamut, chopped parsley, chopped mint, diced cherry tomatoes, red onion, and cucumber.

Prepare Dressing:
- In a small bowl, whisk together the extra virgin olive oil, fresh lemon juice, ground cumin, salt, and black pepper.

Toss Salad:
- Pour the dressing over the kamut and vegetable mixture. Toss the salad gently to ensure all ingredients are well-coated.

Chill:
- Refrigerate the kamut tabbouleh salad for at least 30 minutes to let the flavors meld.

Serve:
- Serve the kamut tabbouleh salad chilled, either as a refreshing side dish or a light and wholesome main course.

Optional Garnish:
- Optionally, garnish with additional fresh mint leaves before serving.

Enjoy this Lebanese-inspired Kamut Tabbouleh Salad, a nutritious and flavorful dish that showcases the unique texture and taste of kamut wheat combined with the vibrant flavors of fresh herbs and vegetables.

Soba Noodle Stir-Fry with Tofu (Japan)

Ingredients:

- 8 oz (about 225g) soba noodles
- 1 block firm tofu, pressed and cubed
- 2 tablespoons soy sauce
- 2 tablespoons mirin
- 1 tablespoon sake (optional)
- 1 tablespoon sesame oil
- 1 tablespoon vegetable oil
- 2 cloves garlic, minced
- 1 tablespoon ginger, grated
- 1 carrot, julienned
- 1 bell pepper, thinly sliced
- 1 cup broccoli florets
- 2 green onions, sliced diagonally
- 1 tablespoon sesame seeds (for garnish)
- Lime wedges (for serving)

Instructions:

Cook Soba Noodles:
- Cook the soba noodles according to the package instructions. Drain, rinse under cold water, and set aside.

Prepare Tofu:
- Press the tofu to remove excess water, then cut it into cubes.

Marinate Tofu:
- In a bowl, combine soy sauce, mirin, and sake (if using). Add the tofu cubes to the marinade, ensuring they are well-coated. Let it marinate for at least 15-20 minutes.

Stir-Fry Tofu:
- Heat vegetable oil in a wok or large skillet over medium-high heat. Add the marinated tofu cubes and stir-fry until golden brown on all sides. Remove tofu from the pan and set aside.

Prepare Vegetables:
- In the same pan, add sesame oil. Add minced garlic and grated ginger. Stir-fry for about 30 seconds until fragrant.

- Add julienned carrot, sliced bell pepper, and broccoli florets to the pan. Stir-fry for 3-4 minutes until the vegetables are crisp-tender.

Combine and Stir-Fry:
- Add the cooked soba noodles and tofu back into the pan with the vegetables.
- Pour the remaining marinade over the noodles and tofu. Toss everything together to combine and heat through.

Serve:
- Divide the soba noodle stir-fry with tofu and vegetables among serving plates.
- Garnish with sliced green onions and sesame seeds.
- Serve hot with lime wedges on the side.

Enjoy:
- Enjoy this Japanese-inspired soba noodle stir-fry with tofu as a delicious and satisfying meal that combines the earthy flavors of soba noodles with the protein-rich goodness of tofu and an assortment of colorful vegetables.

Amaranth and Sweet Potato Patties (Latin America)

Ingredients:

- 1 cup amaranth, cooked
- 2 cups sweet potatoes, mashed
- 1 cup black beans, cooked and mashed
- 1/2 cup red onion, finely chopped
- 2 cloves garlic, minced
- 1 teaspoon ground cumin
- 1 teaspoon chili powder
- 1/2 teaspoon smoked paprika
- Salt and black pepper to taste
- 1/4 cup cilantro, finely chopped
- 1/2 cup breadcrumbs (plus extra for coating)
- 2 tablespoons olive oil (for frying)

Instructions:

Prepare Amaranth:
- Cook amaranth according to package instructions. Once cooked, set aside to cool.

Cook Sweet Potatoes:
- Peel, cube, and boil sweet potatoes until tender. Mash them in a bowl and set aside to cool.

Mash Black Beans:
- In a separate bowl, mash the black beans using a fork or potato masher.

Mix Ingredients:
- In a large mixing bowl, combine the cooked amaranth, mashed sweet potatoes, mashed black beans, finely chopped red onion, minced garlic, ground cumin, chili powder, smoked paprika, salt, black pepper, and chopped cilantro. Mix well.

Add Breadcrumbs:
- Stir in the breadcrumbs until the mixture comes together and is easy to handle.

Shape Patties:
- Divide the mixture into equal portions and shape them into patties.

Coat in Breadcrumbs:

- Coat each patty with additional breadcrumbs, ensuring an even coating on both sides.

Pan-Fry:
- Heat olive oil in a skillet over medium heat. Fry the amaranth and sweet potato patties until golden brown on both sides, about 3-4 minutes per side.

Serve:
- Remove the patties from the skillet and place them on a plate lined with paper towels to absorb any excess oil.

Enjoy:
- Serve these Latin American-inspired amaranth and sweet potato patties hot, perhaps with a side of avocado salsa or your favorite dipping sauce.

These delicious and nutritious patties showcase the versatility of amaranth and the delightful combination of sweet potatoes and black beans, creating a flavorful and satisfying dish inspired by Latin American culinary traditions.

Sorghum Porridge with Berries (Africa)

Ingredients:

- 1 cup sorghum grains, rinsed
- 3 cups water
- 1 cup milk (dairy or plant-based)
- 2 tablespoons honey or maple syrup (adjust to taste)
- 1/2 teaspoon ground cinnamon
- 1/4 teaspoon salt
- 1 cup mixed berries (strawberries, blueberries, raspberries)
- 2 tablespoons chopped nuts (such as almonds or walnuts, optional)
- Fresh mint leaves for garnish (optional)

Instructions:

Cook Sorghum:
- In a medium-sized saucepan, combine the rinsed sorghum grains and water. Bring to a boil, then reduce the heat to low, cover, and simmer for 40-45 minutes or until the sorghum is tender. Drain any excess water.

Add Milk and Sweetener:
- Pour in the milk of your choice into the cooked sorghum. Add honey or maple syrup, ground cinnamon, and salt. Stir well and let it simmer for an additional 5-7 minutes until the porridge thickens.

Prepare Berries:
- While the porridge is simmering, wash and chop the mixed berries.

Serve:
- Spoon the sorghum porridge into serving bowls.
- Top the porridge with a generous portion of mixed berries.
- Optionally, sprinkle chopped nuts over the berries.

Garnish:
- Garnish with fresh mint leaves for a burst of freshness.

Enjoy:
- Serve this African-inspired sorghum porridge with berries warm. The combination of hearty sorghum and vibrant berries creates a nutritious and flavorful dish, perfect for a wholesome breakfast or comforting snack.

Freekeh and Roasted Vegetable Skewers (Middle East)

Ingredients:

- 1 cup freekeh, rinsed and drained
- 2 cups vegetable broth or water
- 1 red bell pepper, cut into chunks
- 1 yellow bell pepper, cut into chunks
- 1 zucchini, sliced into rounds
- 1 red onion, cut into chunks
- Cherry tomatoes
- 3 tablespoons olive oil
- 2 tablespoons lemon juice
- 2 cloves garlic, minced
- 1 teaspoon ground cumin
- 1 teaspoon ground coriander
- 1 teaspoon paprika
- Salt and black pepper to taste
- Wooden skewers, soaked in water for 30 minutes

Instructions:

Prepare Freekeh:
- In a saucepan, combine the rinsed freekeh and vegetable broth or water. Bring to a boil, then reduce the heat to low, cover, and simmer for 20-25 minutes or until the freekeh is tender. Drain any excess liquid and let it cool.

Marinate Vegetables:
- In a bowl, whisk together olive oil, lemon juice, minced garlic, ground cumin, ground coriander, paprika, salt, and black pepper.
- Add the prepared vegetables to the marinade, tossing to coat them evenly. Let them marinate for at least 15-20 minutes.

Assemble Skewers:
- Preheat the grill or oven to medium-high heat.
- Thread the marinated vegetables and cooked freekeh onto the soaked wooden skewers, alternating between vegetables and freekeh.

Grill or Roast:

- Grill the skewers for about 10-15 minutes, turning occasionally, until the vegetables are tender and slightly charred.
- Alternatively, you can roast the skewers in the oven at 400°F (200°C) for 15-20 minutes, or until the vegetables are cooked to your liking.

Serve:
- Once done, remove the skewers from the grill or oven.
- Serve the freekeh and roasted vegetable skewers hot, either as a side dish or a light main course.

Enjoy:
- Enjoy these Middle Eastern-inspired skewers, where the nutty flavor of freekeh complements the smoky taste of the grilled or roasted vegetables. It's a delightful and nutritious dish that captures the essence of Middle Eastern cuisine.

Polenta with Roasted Vegetables and Pesto (Italy)

Ingredients:

For the Polenta:

- 1 cup polenta
- 4 cups vegetable broth or water
- Salt and black pepper to taste
- 1/2 cup grated Parmesan cheese (optional)
- 2 tablespoons unsalted butter (optional)

For the Roasted Vegetables:

- 1 zucchini, sliced
- 1 yellow bell pepper, sliced
- 1 red onion, sliced
- Cherry tomatoes
- 3 tablespoons olive oil
- 2 cloves garlic, minced
- 1 teaspoon dried thyme
- Salt and black pepper to taste

For the Pesto:

- 2 cups fresh basil leaves
- 1/2 cup pine nuts
- 1/2 cup grated Parmesan cheese
- 2 cloves garlic
- 1/2 cup extra virgin olive oil
- Salt and black pepper to taste
- Juice of 1 lemon (optional)

Instructions:

Prepare Polenta:

In a medium saucepan, bring the vegetable broth or water to a boil. Gradually whisk in the polenta, stirring continuously to avoid lumps.

Reduce the heat to low, and continue to cook the polenta, stirring frequently, for about 20-25 minutes or until it becomes thick and creamy.

Season with salt and black pepper. If desired, stir in grated Parmesan cheese and butter for extra richness.

Roast Vegetables:

Preheat the oven to 400°F (200°C).

In a large bowl, toss the sliced zucchini, yellow bell pepper, red onion, and cherry tomatoes with olive oil, minced garlic, dried thyme, salt, and black pepper.

Spread the vegetables on a baking sheet in a single layer.

Roast in the preheated oven for 20-25 minutes or until the vegetables are tender and slightly caramelized.

Prepare Pesto:

In a food processor, combine fresh basil leaves, pine nuts, grated Parmesan cheese, and garlic.

Pulse until the ingredients are finely chopped.

With the processor running, slowly pour in the olive oil until the pesto reaches your desired consistency.

Season with salt and black pepper. Optionally, add lemon juice for a hint of acidity.

Assemble the Dish:

Spoon the creamy polenta onto serving plates.

Top with the roasted vegetables.

Drizzle the fresh pesto over the vegetables and polenta.

Optionally, garnish with additional Parmesan cheese and a sprinkle of fresh basil.

Serve immediately and enjoy this Italian-inspired dish of polenta with roasted vegetables and pesto, showcasing a delightful combination of flavors and textures.

Barley and Mushroom Risotto (Europe)

Ingredients:

- 1 cup pearl barley
- 4 cups vegetable broth, kept warm
- 2 tablespoons olive oil
- 1 onion, finely chopped
- 2 cloves garlic, minced
- 8 oz (about 225g) mushrooms (such as cremini or shiitake), sliced
- 1 cup dry white wine
- 1/2 cup Parmesan cheese, grated
- Salt and black pepper to taste
- Fresh parsley, chopped (for garnish)

Instructions:

Prepare Barley:
- In a large saucepan, heat olive oil over medium heat. Add chopped onion and garlic. Sauté until softened.

Sauté Mushrooms:
- Add sliced mushrooms to the pan. Cook until they release their moisture and become golden brown.

Add Barley:
- Stir in the pearl barley, coating it with the onion, garlic, and mushroom mixture.

Deglaze with Wine:
- Pour in the dry white wine, stirring continuously. Allow the wine to cook off, leaving a rich flavor in the barley.

Start Adding Broth:
- Begin adding the warm vegetable broth one ladle at a time, stirring frequently. Allow the liquid to be absorbed before adding the next ladle.

Continue Cooking:
- Continue this process until the barley is cooked al dente. This may take around 30-40 minutes.

Finish with Cheese:
- Once the barley is cooked to your liking, stir in the grated Parmesan cheese. Season with salt and black pepper to taste.

Garnish and Serve:

- Garnish the barley and mushroom risotto with chopped fresh parsley.
- Serve the risotto hot, offering a comforting and hearty European-inspired dish that showcases the nutty flavor of barley combined with the earthiness of mushrooms.

Enjoy this unique twist on traditional risotto with the wholesome goodness of barley and the rich umami taste of mushrooms!

Quinoa-Stuffed Bell Peppers (South America)

Ingredients:

- 1 cup quinoa, rinsed
- 2 cups vegetable broth
- 4 large bell peppers (any color)
- 1 can (15 oz) black beans, drained and rinsed
- 1 cup corn kernels (fresh or frozen)
- 1 cup cherry tomatoes, diced
- 1/2 red onion, finely chopped
- 2 cloves garlic, minced
- 1 teaspoon ground cumin
- 1 teaspoon chili powder
- 1/2 teaspoon paprika
- Salt and black pepper to taste
- 1 cup shredded cheese (cheddar, Monterey Jack, or a blend)
- Fresh cilantro, chopped (for garnish)
- Lime wedges (for serving)

Instructions:

Cook Quinoa:
- In a medium saucepan, combine the quinoa and vegetable broth. Bring to a boil, then reduce the heat to low, cover, and simmer for about 15-20 minutes or until the quinoa is cooked and the liquid is absorbed. Fluff the quinoa with a fork and set aside.

Prepare Bell Peppers:
- Preheat the oven to 375°F (190°C).
- Cut the tops off the bell peppers and remove the seeds and membranes.

Saute Vegetable Filling:
- In a large skillet, heat olive oil over medium heat. Add chopped red onion and minced garlic. Sauté until softened.

Add Vegetables and Seasonings:
- Add black beans, corn, diced cherry tomatoes, ground cumin, chili powder, paprika, salt, and black pepper to the skillet. Stir well and cook for an additional 3-5 minutes until the vegetables are tender.

Combine with Quinoa:

- Add the cooked quinoa to the vegetable mixture. Mix thoroughly, ensuring all ingredients are well combined.

Stuff Bell Peppers:
- Stuff each bell pepper with the quinoa and vegetable mixture, pressing down gently to pack the filling.

Top with Cheese:
- Sprinkle shredded cheese over the top of each stuffed pepper.

Bake:
- Place the stuffed peppers in a baking dish and bake in the preheated oven for 25-30 minutes or until the peppers are tender and the cheese is melted and bubbly.

Garnish and Serve:
- Remove from the oven and let them cool slightly.
- Garnish with chopped fresh cilantro and serve with lime wedges on the side.

Enjoy:
- Enjoy these South American-inspired quinoa-stuffed bell peppers as a vibrant and nutritious dish, combining the wholesome goodness of quinoa with a variety of flavorful vegetables.

Millet Porridge with Coconut Milk (Asia)

Ingredients:

- 1 cup millet, rinsed and drained
- 2 cups water
- 1 can (14 oz) coconut milk
- 2 tablespoons honey or sweetener of choice
- 1/2 teaspoon vanilla extract
- Pinch of salt
- Fresh fruits for topping (such as sliced mango, banana, or berries)
- Toasted coconut flakes (for garnish)
- Chopped nuts (such as almonds or cashews, optional)

Instructions:

Cook Millet:
- In a medium-sized saucepan, combine the rinsed millet and water. Bring to a boil, then reduce the heat to low, cover, and simmer for about 20-25 minutes or until the millet is cooked and has absorbed most of the water.

Add Coconut Milk:
- Pour in the coconut milk, honey (or sweetener), vanilla extract, and a pinch of salt. Stir well to combine.

Simmer:
- Continue to simmer the millet porridge over low heat for an additional 10-15 minutes, stirring occasionally, until it reaches a creamy consistency.

Adjust Sweetness:
- Taste the porridge and adjust the sweetness if needed by adding more honey or sweetener.

Serve:
- Ladle the millet porridge into bowls.

Top with Fresh Fruits:
- Garnish with a variety of fresh fruits, such as sliced mango, banana, or berries.

Add Crunchy Toppings:
- Optionally, sprinkle toasted coconut flakes and chopped nuts (such as almonds or cashews) over the top for added texture and flavor.

Enjoy:

- Serve this Asian-inspired millet porridge with coconut milk warm, savoring the delightful combination of creamy millet, rich coconut milk, and the natural sweetness of fresh fruits.

Buckwheat Galettes with Ham and Cheese (France)

Inspired by French cuisine

Buckwheat Galette Batter:

- 1 cup buckwheat flour
- 1 1/2 cups water
- 1/2 teaspoon salt
- 1 large egg

Filling:

- 4 slices of ham
- 1 cup grated Gruyère or Emmental cheese
- 1 tablespoon butter
- Freshly ground black pepper
- Chopped fresh parsley for garnish (optional)

Instructions:

Prepare Buckwheat Galette Batter:

In a mixing bowl, combine buckwheat flour and salt.
Gradually whisk in water to avoid lumps. Add the egg and continue whisking until you have a smooth batter.
Allow the batter to rest for at least 30 minutes to 1 hour to let the flavors meld.

Cook Galettes:

Heat a non-stick skillet or a crepe pan over medium-high heat.
Brush the pan with a little butter or oil.
Pour a ladleful of buckwheat batter into the center of the pan, swirling it around to spread it thinly and evenly.
Cook for 2-3 minutes or until the edges start to crisp up and the bottom is golden brown. Flip the galette and cook for an additional 1-2 minutes on the other side.
Repeat until all the batter is used, stacking the cooked galettes on a plate.

Assemble Buckwheat Galettes:

Preheat the oven broiler.
Place a galette on a baking sheet.
Lay a slice of ham on one-half of the galette.
Sprinkle grated cheese over the ham.
Fold the other half of the galette over the filling, creating a half-moon shape.
Repeat the process for the remaining galettes.
Dot the tops with a little butter and place under the broiler until the cheese is melted and bubbly, and the galettes are lightly browned.
Remove from the oven, sprinkle with freshly ground black pepper, and garnish with chopped fresh parsley if desired.

Serve:

- Serve the buckwheat galettes with ham and cheese immediately while hot.
- Enjoy this classic French dish as a delightful and savory treat, perfect for a meal any time of the day!

Sesame Seared Tofu with Brown Rice (Asia)

Ingredients:

For the Sesame Seared Tofu:

- 1 block firm tofu, pressed and cut into cubes
- 2 tablespoons soy sauce
- 1 tablespoon sesame oil
- 1 tablespoon rice vinegar
- 1 tablespoon maple syrup or agave nectar
- 1 tablespoon sesame seeds
- 2 tablespoons cornstarch
- 2 tablespoons vegetable oil (for searing)

For the Brown Rice:

- 1 cup brown rice, rinsed
- 2 cups water
- Pinch of salt

For Garnish:

- Sliced green onions
- Sesame seeds
- Chopped cilantro

Instructions:

Prepare Brown Rice:

In a medium saucepan, combine the rinsed brown rice, water, and a pinch of salt. Bring to a boil, then reduce the heat to low, cover, and simmer for 40-45 minutes or until the rice is tender and water is absorbed.
Fluff the rice with a fork and let it sit covered for a few minutes before serving.

Prepare Sesame Seared Tofu:

In a bowl, whisk together soy sauce, sesame oil, rice vinegar, and maple syrup.
Add the tofu cubes to the marinade, ensuring they are well-coated. Let them marinate for at least 15-20 minutes.
In a separate bowl, combine sesame seeds and cornstarch.
Gently toss the marinated tofu cubes in the sesame seed and cornstarch mixture until evenly coated.
Heat vegetable oil in a skillet or wok over medium-high heat.
Sear the tofu cubes on all sides until golden brown and crispy, about 3-4 minutes per side.
Remove the tofu from the skillet and place them on a plate lined with paper towels to absorb any excess oil.

Assemble:

Serve the sesame seared tofu over a bed of cooked brown rice.
Garnish with sliced green onions, additional sesame seeds, and chopped cilantro.
Optionally, drizzle with extra soy sauce or your favorite Asian-inspired sauce.
Enjoy this Asian-inspired sesame seared tofu with brown rice as a flavorful and protein-packed meal!

Farro and Roasted Beet Salad (Italy)

Ingredients:

For the Salad:

- 1 cup farro, rinsed
- 3 cups water
- 3 medium-sized beets, peeled and diced
- 1 tablespoon olive oil
- Salt and black pepper to taste
- 1/2 cup feta cheese, crumbled
- 1/4 cup chopped fresh parsley

For the Dressing:

- 3 tablespoons balsamic vinegar
- 2 tablespoons extra virgin olive oil
- 1 tablespoon honey or maple syrup
- 1 teaspoon Dijon mustard
- Salt and black pepper to taste

Optional Toppings:

- Toasted walnuts or pecans
- Arugula leaves

Instructions:

Prepare Farro:

In a medium saucepan, combine the rinsed farro and water. Bring to a boil, then reduce the heat to low, cover, and simmer for 25-30 minutes or until the farro is tender but still chewy. Drain any excess water.

Roast Beets:

Preheat the oven to 400°F (200°C).
Toss the diced beets with olive oil, salt, and black pepper.
Spread the beets on a baking sheet in a single layer.
Roast in the preheated oven for 20-25 minutes or until the beets are tender and slightly caramelized.

Prepare Dressing:

In a small bowl, whisk together balsamic vinegar, extra virgin olive oil, honey (or maple syrup), Dijon mustard, salt, and black pepper.

Assemble Salad:

In a large bowl, combine the cooked farro, roasted beets, crumbled feta cheese, and chopped fresh parsley.
Drizzle the dressing over the salad and toss gently to combine, ensuring everything is well coated.
If desired, add optional toppings like toasted walnuts or pecans and arugula leaves.

Serve:

Spoon the farro and roasted beet salad onto serving plates or a large platter.
Serve at room temperature or chilled.
Enjoy this Italian-inspired farro and roasted beet salad as a hearty and nutritious dish, showcasing the earthy flavors of farro and the vibrant colors of roasted beets.

Spelt Bread with Avocado and Tomato (Europe)

Ingredients:

- 4 slices of spelt bread
- 2 ripe avocados
- 1 large tomato, sliced
- 1 tablespoon lemon juice
- Salt and black pepper to taste
- Red pepper flakes (optional, for a bit of heat)
- Olive oil for drizzling
- Fresh basil leaves for garnish (optional)

Instructions:

Prepare Avocado Spread:
- In a bowl, mash the ripe avocados with a fork.
- Add lemon juice, salt, black pepper, and red pepper flakes (if using). Mix well to create a smooth avocado spread.

Toast Spelt Bread:
- Toast the spelt bread slices to your desired level of crispiness.

Assemble the Sandwich:
- Spread the mashed avocado generously on each slice of toasted spelt bread.
- Arrange tomato slices on top of the avocado spread.
- Drizzle olive oil over the tomatoes and sprinkle with additional salt and black pepper.

Garnish:
- Garnish the sandwiches with fresh basil leaves if desired.

Serve:
- Serve the spelt bread with avocado and tomato sandwiches immediately.

Enjoy:
- Enjoy this European-inspired sandwich as a light and satisfying meal, highlighting the wholesome goodness of spelt bread, creamy avocado, and juicy tomatoes.

Teff Porridge with Berries and Almonds (Ethiopia)

Ingredients:

- 1 cup teff grains
- 3 cups water
- 1 cup mixed berries (strawberries, blueberries, raspberries)
- 1/4 cup sliced almonds
- 2 tablespoons honey or maple syrup (adjust to taste)
- 1/2 teaspoon ground cinnamon
- Pinch of salt
- Coconut milk or yogurt (optional, for serving)

Instructions:

Cook Teff:
- In a medium-sized saucepan, combine the teff grains and water. Bring to a boil, then reduce the heat to low, cover, and simmer for about 15-20 minutes or until the teff is cooked and has a porridge-like consistency. Stir occasionally to prevent sticking.

Prepare Berries:
- While the teff is cooking, wash and chop the mixed berries.

Add Sweetener and Spice:
- Once the teff is cooked, add honey (or maple syrup), ground cinnamon, and a pinch of salt. Stir well to combine.

Serve:
- Spoon the teff porridge into serving bowls.
- Top the porridge with the mixed berries and sliced almonds.

Optional:
- Optionally, drizzle coconut milk or add a dollop of yogurt on top for extra creaminess.

Enjoy:
- Enjoy this Ethiopian-inspired teff porridge with berries and almonds as a wholesome and nutritious breakfast or snack, featuring the unique flavors and textures of teff, paired with the natural sweetness of berries and the crunch of sliced almonds.

Amaranth and Spinach Stuffed Mushrooms (Global)

Ingredients:

- 12 large mushrooms, cleaned and stems removed
- 1/2 cup amaranth, cooked
- 1 cup fresh spinach, chopped
- 1/2 cup feta cheese, crumbled
- 1/4 cup grated Parmesan cheese
- 2 cloves garlic, minced
- 1 tablespoon olive oil
- 1 tablespoon fresh lemon juice
- Salt and black pepper to taste
- Fresh parsley for garnish

Instructions:

Preheat the Oven:
- Preheat your oven to 375°F (190°C).

Prepare Mushrooms:
- Place the cleaned mushrooms on a baking sheet.

Prepare Filling:
- In a pan, heat olive oil over medium heat. Add minced garlic and cook until fragrant.
- Add chopped spinach to the pan and cook until wilted.
- In a bowl, combine cooked amaranth, sautéed spinach, crumbled feta cheese, grated Parmesan, and fresh lemon juice. Mix well.

Season:
- Season the filling with salt and black pepper according to your taste.

Stuff Mushrooms:
- Generously stuff each mushroom cap with the amaranth and spinach mixture.

Bake:
- Place the stuffed mushrooms in the preheated oven and bake for 15-20 minutes or until the mushrooms are tender and the filling is golden brown.

Garnish:
- Remove the stuffed mushrooms from the oven. Garnish with fresh parsley.

Serve:

- Serve these amaranth and spinach stuffed mushrooms as a delightful appetizer or a flavorful side dish.

Enjoy:
- Enjoy these globally inspired stuffed mushrooms, combining the nutty flavor of amaranth with the freshness of spinach, creating a delicious and wholesome dish that can be appreciated across various culinary traditions.

Wild Rice and Cranberry Pilaf (North America)

Ingredients:

- 1 cup wild rice, rinsed
- 3 cups vegetable or chicken broth
- 1/2 cup dried cranberries
- 1/2 cup pecans, chopped
- 1 small onion, finely chopped
- 2 cloves garlic, minced
- 2 tablespoons olive oil
- 1 teaspoon dried thyme
- Salt and black pepper to taste
- Chopped fresh parsley for garnish (optional)
- Orange zest for garnish (optional)

Instructions:

Cook Wild Rice:
- In a medium saucepan, combine the rinsed wild rice and broth. Bring to a boil, then reduce the heat to low, cover, and simmer for about 45-50 minutes or until the wild rice is tender and has popped open. Drain any excess liquid.

Prepare Cranberries:
- In a small bowl, soak the dried cranberries in hot water for about 10 minutes to plump them up. Drain and set aside.

Saute Onion and Garlic:
- In a large skillet, heat olive oil over medium heat. Add finely chopped onion and sauté until translucent.
- Add minced garlic to the skillet and cook for an additional 1-2 minutes until fragrant.

Toast Pecans:
- Stir in the chopped pecans and toast them for 2-3 minutes until they become fragrant and lightly browned.

Combine and Season:
- Add the cooked wild rice and plumped cranberries to the skillet. Stir to combine.

- Season the pilaf with dried thyme, salt, and black pepper. Adjust the seasoning to your taste.

Garnish:
- Garnish the wild rice and cranberry pilaf with chopped fresh parsley and a sprinkle of orange zest for added brightness (optional).

Serve:
- Spoon the pilaf onto a serving dish or individual plates.

Enjoy:
- Enjoy this North American-inspired wild rice and cranberry pilaf as a flavorful and festive side dish, combining the earthy notes of wild rice with the sweet-tart flavor of cranberries and the crunch of toasted pecans.

Sorghum and Vegetable Curry (Africa)

Ingredients:

- 1 cup sorghum grains, rinsed and drained
- 3 cups vegetable broth or water
- 2 tablespoons vegetable oil
- 1 large onion, finely chopped
- 3 cloves garlic, minced
- 1 tablespoon ginger, grated
- 1 tablespoon curry powder
- 1 teaspoon ground cumin
- 1 teaspoon ground coriander
- 1/2 teaspoon turmeric
- 1/4 teaspoon cayenne pepper (adjust to taste)
- 1 can (14 oz) chickpeas, drained and rinsed
- 1 cup sweet potatoes, peeled and diced
- 1 cup carrots, sliced
- 1 cup bell peppers, diced (use a mix of colors)
- 1 can (14 oz) diced tomatoes
- 1 can (14 oz) coconut milk
- Salt and black pepper to taste
- Fresh cilantro, chopped (for garnish)
- Cooked rice or flatbread (for serving)

Instructions:

Cook Sorghum:
- In a large pot, combine the rinsed sorghum grains and vegetable broth or water. Bring to a boil, then reduce the heat to low, cover, and simmer for about 50-60 minutes or until the sorghum is tender. Drain any excess liquid.

Prepare Vegetables:
- In a large, deep skillet or pot, heat vegetable oil over medium heat. Add chopped onion and sauté until softened.
- Add minced garlic and grated ginger to the skillet. Cook for an additional 1-2 minutes until fragrant.

- Stir in curry powder, ground cumin, ground coriander, turmeric, and cayenne pepper. Cook for another 2-3 minutes to toast the spices.

Add Vegetables and Chickpeas:
- Add diced sweet potatoes, sliced carrots, diced bell peppers, chickpeas, and diced tomatoes (with their juice) to the skillet. Stir well to coat the vegetables in the spice mixture.

Simmer:
- Pour in the coconut milk and bring the mixture to a simmer. Let it cook for about 15-20 minutes or until the vegetables are tender.

Combine Sorghum and Curry:
- Add the cooked sorghum to the curry mixture. Stir to combine and allow the flavors to meld for an additional 5-10 minutes.

Season:
- Season the curry with salt and black pepper to taste. Adjust the spice leve if needed.

Serve:
- Serve the sorghum and vegetable curry over cooked rice or with flatbread.

Garnish:
- Garnish with chopped fresh cilantro before serving.

Enjoy:
- Enjoy this African-inspired sorghum and vegetable curry, rich in flavors and textures, as a wholesome and satisfying meal.

Quinoa and Black Bean Enchiladas (Latin America)

Ingredients:

For the Filling:

- 1 cup quinoa, rinsed
- 2 cups vegetable broth
- 1 can (15 oz) black beans, drained and rinsed
- 1 cup corn kernels (fresh or frozen)
- 1 red bell pepper, diced
- 1 small red onion, finely chopped
- 2 cloves garlic, minced
- 1 teaspoon ground cumin
- 1 teaspoon chili powder
- Salt and black pepper to taste
- 1 cup shredded cheese (cheddar, Monterey Jack, or a blend)

For the Enchilada Sauce:

- 2 cups tomato sauce
- 1 tablespoon olive oil
- 1 teaspoon ground cumin
- 1 teaspoon chili powder
- 1/2 teaspoon garlic powder
- Salt and black pepper to taste

For Assembly:

- 10-12 corn tortillas
- 1 cup shredded cheese (for topping)
- Fresh cilantro, chopped (for garnish)
- Avocado slices (for serving)

Instructions:

Prepare Quinoa:

In a medium saucepan, combine quinoa and vegetable broth. Bring to a boil, then reduce heat to low, cover, and simmer for 15-20 minutes or until quinoa is cooked and liquid is absorbed.

Prepare Filling:

Preheat the oven to 375°F (190°C).
In a large bowl, combine cooked quinoa, black beans, corn, diced red bell pepper, chopped red onion, minced garlic, ground cumin, chili powder, salt, and black pepper. Mix well.
Stir in the shredded cheese until evenly distributed throughout the filling.

Prepare Enchilada Sauce:

In a saucepan, heat olive oil over medium heat. Add ground cumin, chili powder, and garlic powder. Stir for about 1 minute until fragrant.
Pour in the tomato sauce and season with salt and black pepper. Simmer for 5-7 minutes, stirring occasionally.

Assembly:

Warm the corn tortillas slightly.
Spoon a generous portion of the quinoa and black bean filling onto each tortilla, roll it up, and place it seam-side down in a baking dish.
Pour the enchilada sauce over the rolled tortillas, ensuring they are well-covered.
Sprinkle shredded cheese over the top.

Bake:

Bake in the preheated oven for 20-25 minutes or until the cheese is melted and bubbly.

Garnish and Serve:

Remove from the oven and let it cool slightly.
Garnish with chopped fresh cilantro.
Serve the quinoa and black bean enchiladas with avocado slices on the side.

Enjoy:

Enjoy these Latin American-inspired quinoa and black bean enchiladas as a hearty and flavorful meal, bringing together the goodness of quinoa, black beans, and vibrant spices.

Millet and Sweet Potato Patties (Global)

Ingredients:

- 1 cup millet, rinsed
- 2 cups water
- 1 large sweet potato, peeled and grated
- 1 small red onion, finely chopped
- 2 cloves garlic, minced
- 1/2 cup breadcrumbs
- 2 tablespoons ground flaxseeds mixed with 6 tablespoons water (flax egg)
- 1 teaspoon ground cumin
- 1 teaspoon paprika
- Salt and black pepper to taste
- 2 tablespoons olive oil (for cooking)
- Greek yogurt or tahini sauce (for serving)
- Fresh herbs (parsley, cilantro) for garnish

Instructions:

Cook Millet:
- In a medium saucepan, combine millet and water. Bring to a boil, then reduce heat to low, cover, and simmer for 20-25 minutes or until millet is cooked and water is absorbed. Fluff with a fork and let it cool.

Prepare Flax Egg:
- In a small bowl, mix ground flaxseeds with water and let it sit for a few minutes until it forms a gel-like consistency (flax egg).

Prepare Patties:
- In a large bowl, combine cooked millet, grated sweet potato, chopped red onion, minced garlic, breadcrumbs, flax egg, ground cumin, paprika, salt, and black pepper. Mix well to form a cohesive mixture.
- If the mixture is too wet, add more breadcrumbs; if it's too dry, add a splash of water.

Shape Patties:
- Divide the mixture into equal portions and shape them into patties.

Cooking:
- Heat olive oil in a skillet over medium heat.
- Cook the patties for about 4-5 minutes on each side or until golden brown and crispy.

Serve:
- Serve the millet and sweet potato patties with a dollop of Greek yogurt or tahini sauce.

Garnish:
- Garnish with fresh herbs like parsley or cilantro.

Enjoy:
- Enjoy these globally inspired millet and sweet potato patties as a nutritious and flavorful dish that combines the nuttiness of millet with the natural sweetness of sweet potatoes.

Barley and Roasted Vegetable Pizza (Italy)

Ingredients:

For the Pizza Dough:

- 2 1/4 teaspoons (1 packet) active dry yeast
- 1 cup warm water
- 1 teaspoon sugar
- 3 cups barley flour
- 1 teaspoon salt
- 2 tablespoons olive oil

For the Toppings:

- 1 cup tomato sauce
- 1 1/2 cups shredded mozzarella cheese
- 1 zucchini, thinly sliced
- 1 red bell pepper, thinly sliced
- 1 yellow bell pepper, thinly sliced
- 1 red onion, thinly sliced
- 1 cup cherry tomatoes, halved
- 2 tablespoons olive oil
- Salt and black pepper to taste
- Fresh basil leaves for garnish

Instructions:

Prepare Pizza Dough:

> In a small bowl, combine warm water, sugar, and active dry yeast. Let it sit for about 5-10 minutes until it becomes frothy.
> In a large mixing bowl, combine barley flour and salt. Make a well in the center and pour in the yeast mixture and olive oil.
> Mix until the dough comes together, then knead on a floured surface for about 5-7 minutes until it becomes smooth and elastic.

Place the dough in a lightly oiled bowl, cover with a damp cloth, and let it rise in a warm place for 1-2 hours or until it doubles in size.

Roast Vegetables:

Preheat the oven to 400°F (200°C).
Toss zucchini, red bell pepper, yellow bell pepper, and red onion with olive oil, salt, and black pepper.
Spread the vegetables on a baking sheet and roast for about 20-25 minutes or until they are tender and slightly caramelized.

Assemble and Bake:

Preheat the oven to 475°F (245°C).
Roll out the pizza dough on a floured surface to your desired thickness.
Transfer the rolled-out dough to a pizza stone or a baking sheet.
Spread tomato sauce evenly over the dough, leaving a small border around the edges.
Sprinkle shredded mozzarella cheese over the sauce.
Arrange the roasted vegetables and cherry tomatoes on top.
Bake in the preheated oven for 15-20 minutes or until the crust is golden and the cheese is bubbly.

Garnish and Serve:

Remove the pizza from the oven and let it cool for a few minutes.
Garnish with fresh basil leaves.
Slice and serve.

Enjoy:

Enjoy this Italian-inspired barley and roasted vegetable pizza as a delicious and wholesome twist on a classic favorite!

Freekeh and Chickpea Salad (Middle East)

Ingredients:

For the Salad:

- 1 cup freekeh, cooked and cooled
- 1 can (15 oz) chickpeas, drained and rinsed
- 1 cucumber, diced
- 1 tomato, diced
- 1 red onion, finely chopped
- 1/2 cup fresh parsley, chopped
- 1/4 cup fresh mint, chopped
- 1/2 cup feta cheese, crumbled (optional)
- Salt and black pepper to taste

For the Dressing:

- 1/4 cup extra virgin olive oil
- 2 tablespoons lemon juice
- 1 teaspoon ground cumin
- 1 teaspoon ground coriander
- 1 clove garlic, minced
- Salt and black pepper to taste

Instructions:

Prepare Freekeh:

Cook the freekeh according to the package instructions. Once cooked, let it cool to room temperature.

Prepare Chickpeas:

Drain and rinse the canned chickpeas thoroughly.

Assemble Salad:

In a large bowl, combine the cooked and cooled freekeh, chickpeas, diced cucumber, diced tomato, finely chopped red onion, chopped fresh parsley, and chopped fresh mint.

If using, add crumbled feta cheese to the salad.

Season the salad with salt and black pepper according to your taste.

Prepare Dressing:

In a small bowl, whisk together extra virgin olive oil, lemon juice, ground cumin, ground coriander, minced garlic, salt, and black pepper.

Pour the dressing over the salad and toss everything together until well coated.

Allow the salad to sit for a few minutes to let the flavors meld.

Serve:

Serve the freekeh and chickpea salad in a large serving bowl or as individual portions.

Optionally, garnish with additional fresh herbs or a sprinkle of feta cheese.

Enjoy:

Enjoy this Middle Eastern-inspired freekeh and chickpea salad as a nutritious and flavorful dish, perfect for a light lunch or a refreshing side at any gathering!

Buckwheat Soba Noodles with Miso Broth (Japan)

Ingredients:

For the Broth:

- 4 cups vegetable or mushroom broth
- 3 tablespoons white miso paste
- 2 tablespoons soy sauce
- 1 tablespoon mirin (Japanese sweet rice wine)
- 1 tablespoon rice vinegar
- 1 tablespoon sesame oil
- 2 cloves garlic, minced
- 1 teaspoon fresh ginger, grated
- 1 tablespoon green onions, chopped (for garnish)

For the Noodles and Toppings:

- 8 oz (about 225g) buckwheat soba noodles
- 1 cup shiitake mushrooms, sliced
- 1 cup baby spinach leaves
- 1 medium carrot, julienned
- 1 sheet nori (seaweed), shredded
- Sesame seeds for garnish

Instructions:

Prepare Soba Noodles:

Cook the soba noodles according to the package instructions. Drain and rinse under cold water to stop the cooking process. Set aside.

Prepare Miso Broth:

In a pot, combine vegetable or mushroom broth, white miso paste, soy sauce, mirin, rice vinegar, sesame oil, minced garlic, and grated ginger.

Bring the mixture to a gentle simmer over medium heat, stirring to dissolve the miso paste.

Let the broth simmer for about 10-15 minutes to allow the flavors to meld.

Prepare Toppings:

In a separate pan, sauté shiitake mushrooms until they are tender.

Blanch baby spinach in hot water for a minute, then drain.

Julienne the carrot into thin strips.

Assemble:

Divide the cooked soba noodles among serving bowls.

Ladle the miso broth over the noodles.

Arrange the sautéed shiitake mushrooms, blanched spinach, julienned carrots, and shredded nori on top of the noodles.

Garnish and Serve:

Garnish with chopped green onions and sesame seeds.

Serve the buckwheat soba noodles with miso broth immediately.

Enjoy:

Enjoy this Japanese-inspired dish, featuring the earthy flavor of buckwheat soba noodles in a comforting miso broth with a variety of colorful and nutritious toppings.

Spelt and Herb Focaccia Bread (Italy)

Ingredients:

For the Focaccia Dough:

- 2 1/4 teaspoons (1 packet) active dry yeast
- 1 1/4 cups warm water
- 1 teaspoon honey or sugar
- 3 cups spelt flour
- 1 teaspoon salt
- 3 tablespoons olive oil, divided

For the Herb Topping:

- 2 tablespoons fresh rosemary, chopped
- 1 tablespoon fresh thyme leaves
- 2 tablespoons olive oil
- Sea salt flakes

Instructions:

Prepare Focaccia Dough:

> In a small bowl, combine warm water and honey (or sugar). Sprinkle the yeast over the water and let it sit for 5-10 minutes until it becomes frothy.
> In a large mixing bowl, combine spelt flour and salt. Make a well in the center. Pour the yeast mixture and 2 tablespoons of olive oil into the well. Mix until a dough forms.
> Knead the dough on a floured surface for about 5-7 minutes until it becomes smooth and elastic.
> Place the dough in a lightly oiled bowl, cover with a damp cloth, and let it rise in a warm place for 1-2 hours or until it doubles in size.

Preheat the Oven:

> Preheat your oven to 425°F (220°C).

Shape and Rest the Dough:

Punch down the risen dough and transfer it to a parchment-lined baking sheet. Stretch and press the dough evenly into a rectangular or oval shape, about 1/2 inch thick.

Cover the dough with a clean kitchen towel and let it rest for another 15-20 minutes.

Prepare Herb Topping:

In a small bowl, mix together chopped fresh rosemary, fresh thyme leaves, and 2 tablespoons of olive oil.

Assemble and Bake:

Using your fingers, create dimples in the rested dough.

Drizzle the herb and olive oil mixture evenly over the surface of the dough, making sure it gets into the dimples.

Sprinkle sea salt flakes over the top.

Bake in the preheated oven for 20-25 minutes or until the focaccia is golden brown and sounds hollow when tapped.

Cool and Serve:

Allow the spelt and herb focaccia to cool on a wire rack for a few minutes.

Slice and serve warm or at room temperature.

Enjoy:

Enjoy this Italian-inspired spelt and herb focaccia bread as a delightful accompaniment to soups, salads, or as a tasty snack on its own!

Teff Pancakes with Maple Syrup (Ethiopia)

Ingredients:

- 1 cup teff flour
- 1 tablespoon sugar
- 1 teaspoon baking powder
- 1/4 teaspoon salt
- 1 cup milk (dairy or plant-based)
- 1 large egg
- 2 tablespoons melted butter or oil
- 1 teaspoon vanilla extract (optional)
- Maple syrup for serving
- Fresh berries for garnish (optional)

Instructions:

Prepare the Batter:
- In a mixing bowl, whisk together teff flour, sugar, baking powder, and salt.

Mix Wet Ingredients:
- In a separate bowl, whisk together milk, egg, melted butter or oil, and vanilla extract if using.

Combine Wet and Dry Ingredients:
- Pour the wet ingredients into the dry ingredients and stir until just combined. It's okay if there are a few lumps.

Rest the Batter:
- Let the batter rest for 10-15 minutes. This allows the teff flour to absorb the liquid and results in fluffier pancakes.

Cook Pancakes:
- Heat a griddle or non-stick skillet over medium heat. Lightly grease with butter or oil.
- Pour 1/4 cup of batter for each pancake onto the hot griddle.
- Cook until bubbles form on the surface of the pancake, then flip and cook the other side until golden brown.

Serve:
- Stack the teff pancakes on a plate.
- Drizzle with maple syrup and garnish with fresh berries if desired.

Enjoy:

- Enjoy these Ethiopian-inspired teff pancakes as a unique and nutritious twist on a classic breakfast, featuring the distinct flavor of teff flour!

Sorghum and Pumpkin Soup (Africa)

Ingredients:

- 1 cup sorghum grains, rinsed and drained
- 1 tablespoon olive oil
- 1 onion, finely chopped
- 2 cloves garlic, minced
- 1 teaspoon ground cumin
- 1 teaspoon ground coriander
- 1/2 teaspoon ground cinnamon
- 1/4 teaspoon cayenne pepper (adjust to taste)
- 4 cups pumpkin, peeled and diced
- 1 carrot, peeled and chopped
- 1 celery stalk, chopped
- 6 cups vegetable or chicken broth
- Salt and black pepper to taste
- 1 can (14 oz) coconut milk
- Fresh cilantro, chopped (for garnish)
- Pumpkin seeds (pepitas) for garnish

Instructions:

Cook Sorghum:
- In a large pot, combine sorghum grains with 3 cups of water. Bring to a boil, then reduce the heat to low, cover, and simmer for about 45-60 minutes or until the sorghum is cooked but still chewy. Drain any excess liquid.

Sauté Aromatics:
- In the same pot, heat olive oil over medium heat. Add chopped onion and sauté until softened.
- Add minced garlic and cook for an additional minute until fragrant.

Add Spices:
- Stir in ground cumin, ground coriander, ground cinnamon, and cayenne pepper. Cook for 1-2 minutes to toast the spices.

Add Vegetables:
- Add diced pumpkin, chopped carrot, and chopped celery to the pot. Stir to coat the vegetables in the spice mixture.

Pour in Broth:
- Pour in the vegetable or chicken broth, ensuring it covers the vegetables. Bring to a boil, then reduce the heat and let it simmer for about 15-20 minutes or until the vegetables are tender.

Blend the Soup:
- Use an immersion blender to blend the soup until smooth. Alternatively, transfer the soup in batches to a blender, blend, and return it to the pot.

Add Cooked Sorghum:
- Add the cooked sorghum to the soup and stir to combine.

Season and Add Coconut Milk:
- Season the soup with salt and black pepper to taste.
- Pour in the coconut milk and stir well. Let the soup simmer for an additional 5-10 minutes.

Garnish and Serve:
- Ladle the sorghum and pumpkin soup into bowls.
- Garnish with chopped fresh cilantro and pumpkin seeds.

Enjoy:
- Enjoy this African-inspired sorghum and pumpkin soup as a hearty and flavorful dish, showcasing the wholesome goodness of sorghum and the rich, earthy flavors of pumpkin!

Quinoa and Kale Stuffed Bell Peppers (South America)

Ingredients:

- 1 cup quinoa, rinsed
- 2 cups vegetable broth
- 4 large bell peppers, halved and seeds removed
- 1 tablespoon olive oil
- 1 onion, finely chopped
- 2 cloves garlic, minced
- 4 cups kale, stems removed and leaves chopped
- 1 can (15 oz) black beans, drained and rinsed
- 1 can (14 oz) diced tomatoes, drained
- 1 teaspoon ground cumin
- 1 teaspoon smoked paprika
- Salt and black pepper to taste
- 1 cup shredded cheese (cheddar, Monterey Jack, or a blend)
- Fresh cilantro, chopped (for garnish)
- Avocado slices (for serving)

Instructions:

Cook Quinoa:
- In a medium saucepan, combine quinoa and vegetable broth. Bring to a boil, then reduce heat to low, cover, and simmer for 15-20 minutes or until quinoa is cooked and liquid is absorbed. Fluff with a fork.

Prepare Bell Peppers:
- Preheat the oven to 375°F (190°C).
- Cut the bell peppers in half lengthwise, removing the seeds and membranes. Place them in a baking dish.

Sauté Aromatics:
- In a large skillet, heat olive oil over medium heat. Add chopped onion and sauté until softened.
- Add minced garlic to the skillet and cook for an additional 1-2 minutes until fragrant.

Add Kale and Black Beans:
- Add chopped kale to the skillet and cook until wilted.

- Stir in black beans and cook for a few more minutes until everything is well combined.

Season and Combine:
- Add cooked quinoa, diced tomatoes, ground cumin, smoked paprika, salt, and black pepper to the skillet. Mix well to combine all the ingredients.

Stuff Bell Peppers:
- Spoon the quinoa and kale mixture into each bell pepper half, pressing it down slightly.

Bake:
- Sprinkle shredded cheese over the stuffed peppers.
- Bake in the preheated oven for 25-30 minutes or until the peppers are tender, and the cheese is melted and bubbly.

Garnish and Serve:
- Remove from the oven and let them cool for a few minutes.
- Garnish with chopped fresh cilantro and serve with avocado slices on the side.

Enjoy:
- Enjoy these South American-inspired quinoa and kale stuffed bell peppers as a wholesome and flavorful meal, combining the protein-rich quinoa with the vibrant and nutrient-packed kale!

Millet and Black Bean Tacos (Latin America)

Ingredients:

For the Millet:

- 1 cup millet, rinsed
- 2 cups vegetable broth
- 1 teaspoon ground cumin
- 1 teaspoon chili powder
- 1/2 teaspoon garlic powder
- Salt to taste

For the Black Beans:

- 1 can (15 oz) black beans, drained and rinsed
- 1 tablespoon olive oil
- 1 small onion, finely chopped
- 2 cloves garlic, minced
- 1 teaspoon ground cumin
- 1 teaspoon chili powder
- Salt and black pepper to taste

For Tacos:

- Corn or flour tortillas
- Shredded lettuce
- Diced tomatoes
- Salsa or pico de gallo
- Avocado slices
- Fresh cilantro, chopped
- Lime wedges

Instructions:

Prepare Millet:

> In a medium saucepan, combine millet and vegetable broth. Bring to a boil, then reduce heat to low, cover, and simmer for 20-25 minutes or until millet is cooked and liquid is absorbed.

Stir in ground cumin, chili powder, garlic powder, and salt. Fluff the millet with a fork.

Prepare Black Beans:

In a skillet, heat olive oil over medium heat. Add chopped onion and sauté until softened.
Add minced garlic to the skillet and cook for an additional minute until fragrant.
Stir in drained black beans, ground cumin, chili powder, salt, and black pepper.
Cook for 5-7 minutes, mashing some of the beans with a fork or back of a spoon.

Assemble Tacos:

Warm the tortillas in a dry skillet or microwave.
Spoon the cooked millet and black beans onto each tortilla.
Top with shredded lettuce, diced tomatoes, salsa or pico de gallo, avocado slices, and chopped fresh cilantro.
Squeeze lime juice over the top.

Serve:

Serve the millet and black bean tacos immediately, allowing everyone to customize their tacos with their favorite toppings.

Enjoy:

Enjoy these Latin American-inspired millet and black bean tacos as a delicious and satisfying meal, packed with flavor and wholesome ingredients!

Barley and Lentil Stew (Middle East)

Ingredients:

- 1 cup barley, rinsed
- 1 cup brown lentils, rinsed
- 2 tablespoons olive oil
- 1 large onion, finely chopped
- 3 cloves garlic, minced
- 2 carrots, diced
- 2 celery stalks, diced
- 1 can (14 oz) diced tomatoes
- 6 cups vegetable broth
- 1 teaspoon ground cumin
- 1 teaspoon ground coriander
- 1/2 teaspoon ground turmeric
- 1/2 teaspoon smoked paprika
- Salt and black pepper to taste
- 1 cup spinach or kale, chopped
- Fresh parsley, chopped (for garnish)
- Lemon wedges (for serving)

Instructions:

Cook Barley and Lentils:
- In a large pot, combine barley and lentils with 4 cups of vegetable broth. Bring to a boil, then reduce heat to low, cover, and simmer for about 30-40 minutes or until barley and lentils are tender. Drain any excess liquid.

Sauté Aromatics:
- In the same pot, heat olive oil over medium heat. Add chopped onion and sauté until softened.
- Add minced garlic and cook for an additional minute until fragrant.

Add Vegetables:
- Stir in diced carrots and celery. Cook for 5-7 minutes until the vegetables start to soften.

Season:
- Add ground cumin, ground coriander, ground turmeric, smoked paprika, salt, and black pepper to the pot. Stir to coat the vegetables in the spices.

Combine Tomatoes and Broth:
- Add the can of diced tomatoes (with their juice) to the pot. Pour in the remaining 2 cups of vegetable broth.
- Bring the mixture to a simmer and let it cook for about 15-20 minutes.

Add Cooked Barley and Lentils:
- Stir in the cooked barley and lentils into the stew.

Add Greens:
- Add chopped spinach or kale to the pot and let it wilt into the stew.

Adjust Seasoning:
- Taste and adjust the seasoning, adding more salt or pepper if needed.

Serve:
- Ladle the barley and lentil stew into bowls.
- Garnish with chopped fresh parsley.

Serve with Lemon Wedges:
- Serve the stew with lemon wedges on the side for a bright burst of citrus flavor.

Enjoy:
- Enjoy this Middle Eastern-inspired barley and lentil stew as a hearty and wholesome dish, perfect for colder days!

Amaranth and Vegetable Curry (Global)

Ingredients:

- 1 cup amaranth, rinsed
- 2 tablespoons coconut oil
- 1 large onion, finely chopped
- 3 cloves garlic, minced
- 1 tablespoon ginger, grated
- 1 tablespoon curry powder
- 1 teaspoon ground turmeric
- 1 teaspoon ground cumin
- 1 teaspoon ground coriander
- 1 can (14 oz) diced tomatoes
- 1 can (14 oz) coconut milk
- 2 cups mixed vegetables (e.g., carrots, bell peppers, zucchini)
- Salt and black pepper to taste
- Fresh cilantro, chopped (for garnish)
- Cooked rice or naan bread (for serving)

Instructions:

> Cook Amaranth:
> - In a pot, combine amaranth with 2 cups of water. Bring to a boil, then reduce heat to low, cover, and simmer for 15-20 minutes or until amaranth is cooked and water is absorbed.
>
> Sauté Aromatics:
> - In a large skillet or pot, heat coconut oil over medium heat. Add chopped onion and sauté until softened.
> - Add minced garlic and grated ginger to the skillet. Cook for an additional 1-2 minutes until fragrant.
>
> Add Curry Spices:
> - Stir in curry powder, ground turmeric, ground cumin, and ground coriander. Cook for 1-2 minutes to toast the spices.
>
> Combine Tomatoes and Coconut Milk:
> - Add the can of diced tomatoes (with their juice) to the skillet. Pour in the coconut milk. Mix well to combine.
>
> Add Vegetables:

- Add the mixed vegetables to the curry. Simmer for about 10-15 minutes or until the vegetables are tender.

Fold in Cooked Amaranth:
- Stir in the cooked amaranth into the curry. Mix well to combine.

Season:
- Season the curry with salt and black pepper to taste. Adjust the seasoning as needed.

Simmer:
- Let the curry simmer for an additional 5-10 minutes to allow the flavors to meld.

Garnish and Serve:
- Garnish the amaranth and vegetable curry with chopped fresh cilantro.
- Serve over cooked rice or with naan bread.

Enjoy:
- Enjoy this globally inspired amaranth and vegetable curry as a nutritious and flavorful meal that brings together the richness of coconut milk and a blend of aromatic spices!

Farro and Tomato Bruschetta (Italy)

Ingredients:

- 1 cup farro, rinsed and cooked according to package instructions
- 2 cups cherry tomatoes, diced
- 1/4 cup red onion, finely chopped
- 2 cloves garlic, minced
- 1/4 cup fresh basil, chopped
- 3 tablespoons extra-virgin olive oil
- 1 tablespoon balsamic vinegar
- Salt and pepper to taste
- Baguette or rustic bread, sliced
- Olive oil for brushing bread

Instructions:

Cook farro: Rinse the farro under cold water and cook it according to the package instructions. Once cooked, let it cool to room temperature.
Prepare the tomato mixture: In a large bowl, combine the diced cherry tomatoes, red onion, minced garlic, chopped basil, olive oil, balsamic vinegar, salt, and pepper. Mix well and let it sit for about 15 minutes to allow the flavors to meld.
Toast the bread: Preheat your ovens broiler or a grill pan. Brush the bread slices with olive oil on both sides. Toast the slices until they are golden brown and crispy, turning once to ensure both sides are evenly toasted.
Assemble the bruschetta: Once the farro is cooled and the tomato mixture has marinated, combine them in a bowl. Mix well to ensure the farro is evenly coated with the tomato mixture.
Serve: Spoon the farro and tomato mixture onto the toasted bread slices. You can drizzle a bit of extra olive oil on top for added richness. Serve immediately and enjoy!

This Farro and Tomato Bruschetta makes for a delicious appetizer or light meal, perfect for showcasing the vibrant flavors of fresh tomatoes and the heartiness of farro.

Spelt Pasta with Artichoke and Lemon (Italy)

Ingredients:

- 8 oz (about 225g) spelt pasta
- 1 can (14 oz) artichoke hearts, drained and quartered
- Zest of 1 lemon
- Juice of 1 lemon
- 3 tablespoons extra-virgin olive oil
- 2 cloves garlic, minced
- 1/4 cup fresh parsley, chopped
- Salt and pepper to taste
- Grated Parmesan cheese for serving (optional)

Instructions:

Cook the spelt pasta: Bring a large pot of salted water to a boil. Cook the spelt pasta according to the package instructions until al dente. Drain and set aside.
Prepare the artichokes: If using canned artichoke hearts, drain them and cut them into quarters. If using fresh artichokes, trim and clean them, then steam or boil until tender before cutting them into quarters.
Make the lemon and garlic sauce: In a large skillet, heat the olive oil over medium heat. Add the minced garlic and sauté for about 1-2 minutes until fragrant, being careful not to brown the garlic.
Combine the ingredients: Add the quartered artichoke hearts to the skillet, tossing them in the garlic-infused oil. Stir in the lemon zest and lemon juice. Season with salt and pepper to taste. Cook for an additional 2-3 minutes to allow the flavors to meld.
Mix with pasta: Add the cooked spelt pasta to the skillet, tossing it with the artichoke mixture until everything is well combined and heated through. If needed, add a splash of pasta cooking water to create a light sauce.
Finish and serve: Remove the skillet from heat, and sprinkle chopped fresh parsley over the pasta. Toss once more to incorporate the parsley. Optionally, serve with grated Parmesan cheese on top.
Serve immediately: Plate the Spelt Pasta with Artichoke and Lemon, and serve it hot. Enjoy the delightful combination of nutty spelt pasta, tangy lemon, and the earthy taste of artichokes!

This dish is perfect for a quick and tasty weeknight dinner, offering a unique twist with the use of spelt pasta and the bright flavors of lemon and artichoke.

Teff Injera Tacos with Lentils (Ethiopia)

Teff Injera:

Ingredients:

- 1 cup teff flour
- 1 1/2 cups water
- 1/4 teaspoon salt
- Cooking oil for pan

Instructions:

In a bowl, mix the teff flour, water, and salt until well combined. Allow the batter to rest for at least 4 hours or overnight to ferment slightly.
Heat a non-stick skillet over medium heat. Lightly oil the skillet.
Pour a ladle of the teff batter onto the skillet, swirling it to spread evenly. Cook for about 2 minutes until bubbles form on the surface.
Flip and cook for an additional 1-2 minutes. Repeat with the remaining batter.

Lentil Filling:

Ingredients:

- 1 cup lentils, cooked
- 1 onion, finely chopped
- 2 cloves garlic, minced
- 1 teaspoon ground cumin
- 1 teaspoon ground coriander
- Salt and pepper to taste
- Fresh cilantro, chopped

Instructions:

In a pan, sauté the chopped onion and minced garlic until softened.
Add the cooked lentils, ground cumin, ground coriander, salt, and pepper. Cook for an additional 5-7 minutes until the flavors meld.
Stir in fresh cilantro just before turning off the heat.

Assembly:

Additional Ingredients:

- Avocado slices
- Shredded cabbage or lettuce
- Salsa or hot sauce of your choice

Instructions:

> Take a teff injera and place a portion of the lentil filling in the center.
> Top with avocado slices, shredded cabbage or lettuce, and a drizzle of salsa or hot sauce.
> Fold the injera around the filling to form a taco.

Enjoy the unique blend of flavors and textures in these Teff Injera Tacos with Lentils, combining the earthy teff, savory lentils, and vibrant fresh toppings. It's a delicious and culturally inspired dish that brings together the best of Ethiopian and Mexican cuisines.

Buckwheat Blinis with Smoked Salmon (Russia)

Ingredients:

- 1/2 cup buckwheat flour
- 1/2 cup all-purpose flour
- 1 teaspoon baking powder
- 1/2 teaspoon salt
- 1 cup buttermilk
- 1 large egg
- 2 tablespoons melted butter
- Butter or oil for cooking

Instructions:

In a bowl, whisk together the buckwheat flour, all-purpose flour, baking powder, and salt.
In another bowl, whisk together the buttermilk, egg, and melted butter.
Pour the wet ingredients into the dry ingredients and stir until just combined. Let the batter rest for about 15 minutes.
Heat a skillet or griddle over medium heat and lightly grease with butter or oil.
Pour small amounts of batter onto the skillet to form small pancakes (blinis).
Cook until bubbles form on the surface, then flip and cook the other side until golden brown.
Repeat until all the batter is used.

Topping:

Ingredients:

- Smoked salmon slices
- Cream cheese
- Fresh dill, chopped
- Lemon wedges

Assembly:

Once the buckwheat blinis are cooked, let them cool slightly.
Spread a small amount of cream cheese on each blini.
Top each blini with a slice of smoked salmon.
Sprinkle chopped fresh dill over the smoked salmon.

Serve with lemon wedges on the side.

Optional Garnish:

- Red onion slices
- Capers

Enjoy these Buckwheat Blinis with Smoked Salmon as an elegant appetizer or part of a brunch spread. The combination of the slightly nutty flavor of the buckwheat blinis with the richness of smoked salmon is a delightful treat that's sure to impress your guests.

Sorghum and Peanut Stir-Fry (Africa)

Ingredients:

- 1 cup sorghum grains, cooked (according to package instructions)
- 2 tablespoons vegetable oil
- 1 onion, finely chopped
- 2 cloves garlic, minced
- 1 red bell pepper, thinly sliced
- 1 green bell pepper, thinly sliced
- 1 cup snap peas, trimmed
- 1 cup broccoli florets
- 1/2 cup unsalted peanuts
- 2 tablespoons soy sauce
- 1 tablespoon oyster sauce
- 1 tablespoon rice vinegar
- 1 teaspoon sesame oil
- Salt and pepper to taste
- Fresh cilantro for garnish (optional)
- Lime wedges for serving

Instructions:

Cook Sorghum:
- Rinse the sorghum grains under cold water.
- Cook according to package instructions until tender. Set aside.

Prepare the Vegetables:
- In a large skillet or wok, heat the vegetable oil over medium-high heat.
- Add the chopped onion and minced garlic. Sauté until fragrant and the onion is translucent.

Stir-Fry:
- Add the sliced red and green bell peppers, snap peas, and broccoli florets to the skillet. Stir-fry for 3-4 minutes until the vegetables are slightly tender but still crisp.

Add Peanuts:
- Toss in the unsalted peanuts and continue to stir-fry for an additional 2-3 minutes until the peanuts are lightly toasted.

Combine with Sorghum:
- Add the cooked sorghum to the vegetable and peanut mixture. Mix well to combine.

Prepare Sauce:
- In a small bowl, whisk together soy sauce, oyster sauce, rice vinegar, and sesame oil.

Final Touch:
- Pour the sauce over the sorghum and vegetable mixture. Stir to coat everything evenly.
- Season with salt and pepper to taste.

Serve:
- Garnish with fresh cilantro if desired.
- Serve the Sorghum and Peanut Stir-Fry hot, with lime wedges on the side for squeezing over the dish.

This dish is a delightful blend of textures and flavors, showcasing the heartiness of sorghum and the nutty crunch of peanuts, all complemented by the vibrant vegetables and savory sauce. It's a nutritious and satisfying option that reflects the diverse and delicious cuisines found across the African continent.

Quinoa and Roasted Vegetable Buddha Bowl (Global)

Ingredients:

For the Quinoa:

- 1 cup quinoa, rinsed
- 2 cups vegetable broth or water
- Salt to taste

For the Roasted Vegetables:

- 2 cups mixed vegetables (e.g., sweet potatoes, bell peppers, cherry tomatoes, zucchini), chopped
- 2 tablespoons olive oil
- 1 teaspoon dried herbs (such as thyme, rosemary, or oregano)
- Salt and pepper to taste

For the Dressing:

- 3 tablespoons olive oil
- 2 tablespoons balsamic vinegar
- 1 tablespoon Dijon mustard
- 1 clove garlic, minced
- Salt and pepper to taste

For Assembly:

- Fresh greens (e.g., spinach, kale, arugula)
- Avocado slices
- Hummus
- Sesame seeds or nuts for garnish (optional)

Instructions:

Cook Quinoa:
- In a medium saucepan, combine quinoa, vegetable broth or water, and a pinch of salt. Bring to a boil, then reduce heat, cover, and simmer for about 15-20 minutes or until the quinoa is cooked and the liquid is absorbed. Fluff with a fork.

Roast Vegetables:
- Preheat the oven to 400°F (200°C).
- Toss the chopped vegetables with olive oil, dried herbs, salt, and pepper.

- Spread the vegetables in a single layer on a baking sheet.
- Roast for 20-25 minutes or until the vegetables are tender and slightly caramelized.

Prepare Dressing:
- In a small bowl, whisk together olive oil, balsamic vinegar, Dijon mustard, minced garlic, salt, and pepper.

Assemble Buddha Bowl:
- In individual bowls, start with a base of cooked quinoa.
- Arrange a portion of roasted vegetables on one side of the bowl.
- Add a handful of fresh greens on the other side.
- Place avocado slices and a dollop of hummus on top.
- Drizzle the dressing over the bowl.
- Garnish with sesame seeds or nuts if desired

Serve:
- Serve the Quinoa and Roasted Vegetable Buddha Bowl immediately, allowing everyone to mix and enjoy the variety of flavors and textures.

Feel free to customize your Buddha Bowl with additional ingredients like grilled protein, pickled vegetables, or your favorite sauce. This dish is not only delicious but also a visually appealing and balanced meal that reflects the diverse and healthy aspects of global cuisine.

Millet and Banana Breakfast Bowl (Global)

Ingredients:

For the Millet:
- 1 cup millet
- 2 cups water
- Pinch of salt

For the Banana Topping:
- 2 ripe bananas, sliced
- 1 tablespoon honey or maple syrup
- 1 teaspoon ground cinnamon

Additional Toppings:
- Greek yogurt or plant-based yogurt
- Nuts and seeds (e.g., chopped almonds, chia seeds)
- Fresh berries or sliced fruits
- Nut butter (e.g., almond butter, peanut butter)

Instructions:

Cook Millet:
- Rinse the millet under cold water.
- In a saucepan, combine millet, water, and a pinch of salt.
- Bring to a boil, then reduce heat, cover, and simmer for about 15-20 minutes or until the millet is cooked and water is absorbed. Fluff with a fork.

Prepare Banana Topping:
- In a small bowl, combine sliced bananas, honey or maple syrup, and ground cinnamon. Toss gently to coat the bananas.

Assemble Breakfast Bowl:
- Spoon a portion of cooked millet into a bowl.

Add Banana Topping:
- Arrange the banana topping over the millet.

Additional Toppings:
- Add a dollop of Greek yogurt or your favorite plant-based yogurt.
- Sprinkle nuts and seeds over the bowl for crunch and added nutrition.
- Top with fresh berries or sliced fruits.

Drizzle with Nut Butter:
- Drizzle your preferred nut butter (almond butter, peanut butter) over the breakfast bowl.

Optional Extras:
- You can add a sprinkle of additional cinnamon, a drizzle of extra honey or maple syrup, or a handful of granola for extra texture.

Serve:
- Enjoy your Millet and Banana Breakfast Bowl immediately, savoring the combination of flavors and textures.

This breakfast bowl is not only delicious but also provides a good balance of complex carbohydrates, healthy fats, and protein to keep you energized throughout the morning. Feel free to customize it further with your favorite toppings and enjoy a global-inspired, wholesome start to your day!